Where Water Flows

Letters & Rituals to Heal & Uplift the Sacred Child Within

Dr. Gemma Andaya

Illustrations by Willie Maglothin

Paperback: 978-1-956989-44-1
Hardcover: 978-1-956989-45-8

Dedication

This book is dedicated to the direction of the South, **Huitzlampa**, as honored in Aztec tradition. Associated with **Huitzilopochtli**, the revered protector and guide of the Mexica people, the South embodies the element of water, symbolizing renewal and cleansing. It is the direction of youth and children, representing growth, adaptability, and the boundless potential within each of us.

May we all embrace the qualities of water—teachable, moldable, and ever-flowing—reflecting the spirit of the child. Just as water shapes the earth with its persistence and grace, may we allow our inner child to guide us toward renewal and transformation.

To the sacred child within us all—innocent, curious, and resilient—you are honored, you are cherished, you are whole.

Acknowledgements

I would like to extend my heartfelt gratitude to my teachers, guides, ancestors, family, friends, and beloved who have been unwavering supporters throughout the course of writing this book. Your care, encouragement, and insights have been invaluable.

A special shout-out to my daughter, Ava, who has been on her own healing journey as I wrote this book. Many of these letters were written with you in mind, and I am so proud of the courage and growth you embody.

Above all, I honor the Creator and Mother Earth for this human experience. Writing these words has been a blessing and a joy—a small attempt to rebalance and recalibrate some of the harm done to children. May we all remember that children are sacred.

Table of Contents

How to Use This Book 11

A Personal Note. 15

A Sacred Perspective on Trauma and Healing 19

A Prayer for You 21

    LETTER I As You Change: On Growth and Discovery 23

    Journal Prompts 25

    LETTER II Thank You for Choosing Me: You Are an Inspiration . . 31

    Journal Prompts 34

    LETTER III Love Will Remain: On Resilience and Perseverance . . 39

    Journal Prompts 42

    LETTER IV Who Are YOU? On Embracing Individuality 47

    Journal Prompts 50

    LETTER V The World Is Your Oyster: On Dreams and Aspirations . 55

    Journal Prompts 58

    LETTER VI Protect Your Heart: On Joy and Celebration 63

    Journal Prompts 66

    LETTER VII One Foot in Front of the Other: On Surrendering

    to the Process. 71

    Journal Prompts 74

An Invitation to Deepen Communication 79

    The Inner Child Speaks: Guided Prompts. 85

    Reconnecting with Your Inner Child 85

    Giving Your Inner Child a Voice. 92

    Letting Your Inner Child Guide You 97

Final Closure Ritual: Flowing into Wholeness 103

Epilogue: Flowing Forward 107

Introduction

This book, *Where Water Flows: Letters and Rituals for the Sacred Child Within*, is an invitation to reconnect with the sacred child within you—a journey of healing, self-discovery, and transformation. Whether you are revisiting memories of your past, reflecting on your present, or envisioning your future, the letters, journal prompts, and rituals within these pages are designed to nurture your inner child and remind them of inherent worth and offer you a feeling of wholeness.

The themes explored throughout this book—openness, curiosity, adaptability, and emotional flow—are inspired by the direction of the South. In many Indigenous traditions, the South is associated with water, adaptability, and childhood. Water's flow reminds us to remain teachable, open to change, and connected to the sacred wonder of life.

This journey is not limited to the words on these pages. You'll find journal prompts that encourage deep reflection and rituals that invite you to connect with the transformative power of water. These elements work together to create a toolkit for healing and integration—one that you can personalize to meet your unique needs and experiences.

These practices are for anyone seeking healing and reconnection. They are for the child within who longs to be heard, seen, and loved. They are for young adults, adults, and elders navigating their own growth, whether through self-help, plant medicine, counseling, or other spiritual practices. And they are for anyone ready to reclaim their authenticity and step into their full power.

As you journey through this book, remember that healing is not linear—it is cyclical, like water, always moving and evolving. The letters, prompts, and rituals are here to guide you gently, offering tools to help you weave together the many parts of yourself into a harmonious whole. Just as water shapes the Earth with persistence and grace, you too are capable of reshaping your life, honoring your past while stepping courageously into your future.

How to Use This Book

This book is an invitation to reconnect with your inner child and nurture the sacred bond between who you once were and who you are today. Through letters, prompts, and water rituals, you will explore themes of curiosity, emotional flow, adaptability, and renewal—qualities that mirror both water and the sacred child. By engaging with these practices, you cultivate a deeper relationship with yourself, one that allows for healing, playfulness, and wholeness. Here's how to engage with these tools in a way that feels meaningful to you.

1. Create a Sacred Space
Before engaging with this book, take a moment to prepare your surroundings. Light a candle, play soft music, or place a meaningful object nearby to ground yourself. If possible, include a small bowl of water as a symbol of renewal and emotional flow. Let this be a moment to center yourself and invite your inner child into the space.

2. Read with Presence
Read the letters slowly and intentionally, imagining they are written directly to the child within you. Let the words offer love, understanding, and encouragement. As you read, notice any emotions or memories that arise. Visualize your inner child listening with curiosity and trust, feeling deeply seen and heard.

3. Reflect and Journal

Each letter is paired with prompts to help you explore its themes more deeply. Take time to respond to these prompts, letting your thoughts and emotions flow freely. Writing can uncover insights that help you better understand your inner child and the patterns that shape your life. Revisit these prompts over time, allowing them to evolve as you grow.

4. Incorporate Water Rituals

Throughout this book, you'll find water blessing rituals that honor the sacredness of water and its connection to the themes of healing and adaptability. These rituals are simple, intentional acts, such as thanking water before drinking or offering prayers during a bath. Use them to ground yourself and deepen your connection to the natural world and your inner child.

5. Stay Attuned to Your Inner Child

Your inner child is a dynamic part of you, always present and ready to engage. Pay attention to the moments when they might need your support—through emotions, dreams, or reactions that feel out of proportion. Use this book as a tool to nurture this relationship and offer your inner child the love and guidance they deserve.

6. Moving Through the Book

There is no single way to experience *Where Water Flows: Letters and Rituals for the Sacred Child Within*. This book is designed to flow with your unique healing process. Here are different ways to approach it:

- **Go at your own pace** – Move through the letters, journal prompts, and rituals as you feel called. Some reflections may take time, while others may feel immediately resonant. Honor your personal rhythm.

- **A structured journey** – If you prefer a set path, consider dedicating one letter per week or per month. This approach allows time for deeper integration, giving each theme space to unfold in your life.

- **A spontaneous approach** – Open the book at random, as you would with a tarot or oracle card pull, and reflect on the letter or ritual that presents itself. Trust that the message you land on is exactly what you need at that moment.

- **Revisiting over time** – Healing is not linear. Return to these letters, prompts, and rituals as you evolve. The insights you gain today may transform with time, offering new meaning in different phases of your life.

There is no rush in this process—only the invitation to flow. However you choose to engage, trust your intuition and allow this book to serve as a guide to deeper connection, healing, and self-discovery.

7. Share with Care
The work you're doing is deeply personal but sharing it with trusted individuals can be profoundly healing and inspiring.

- **Inspire others:** Share your experiences with friends, family, or communities who are also exploring healing and self-discovery. Your journey may encourage them to reconnect with their own inner child.

- **Practice discernment:** Be mindful of when, where, and with whom you share. Choose safe spaces and people who will honor your vulnerability and hold your story with care.

- **Celebrate together:** If you feel called, invite others to join you in rituals or reflective practices. Sharing rituals, such as offering gratitude to water, can create bonds and deepen connections.

8. Return to These Practices Often

Healing is not linear, and the work you do today may reveal new layers in the future. Return to these letters, prompts, and rituals as companions on your journey. Each reading can bring fresh insights, allowing you to deepen your relationship with your inner child and continue growing.

A Personal Note

We are living through unprecedented times, witnessing significant legal and political shifts that challenge fundamental personal freedoms. Rights concerning bodily autonomy—hard-won by our predecessors—are now under threat. The U.S. Supreme Court's decision in *Dobbs v. Jackson Women's Health Organization* overturned the constitutional right to abortion, impacting personal liberty and privacy. Additionally, recent legislative actions have restricted access to gender-affirming care for transgender individuals, further challenging bodily autonomy. Illegal immigrants and even green card holders are being deported from the U.S.

While these issues may not directly affect every person, the erosion of inclusive laws sets a dangerous precedent. History has shown that when protections for one group are weakened, it opens the door for further rollbacks in civil rights, personal autonomy, and social progress. These developments underscore the importance of remaining vigilant in protecting the rights that previous generations fought so hard to secure.

Born to immigrant parents who courageously started anew in a foreign land, I witnessed firsthand the power of selfless service. My mother, a devoted healer, served a vast Spanish-speaking Hispanic community, many of whom lacked access to conventional healthcare. Through spiritual cleanses and rituals, she provided solace and guidance, embodying a life of prayer and dedication to her faith. Despite the stigma she faced for practicing both Catholicism and Santería, she remained steadfast in her commitment to helping others until the day she passed.

In my work as a psychotherapist, I have been privileged to support individuals from diverse backgrounds as they confront unprocessed, often unconscious trauma. These deep-seated wounds can foster connections with others—both seen and unseen—who share similar pain. Unhealed wounds can act as an energetic magnet, attracting relationships or even spiritual presences that mirror our unresolved suffering. Whether we view this through the lens of psychology, where trauma patterns unconsciously repeat, or through spiritual traditions that recognize the presence of lost or lingering energies, the impact is the same—our pain has a way of seeking recognition. Acknowledging and tending to these wounds is an act of sovereignty, a way of reclaiming our energy and stepping into wholeness, free from cycles of past pain.

I honor both modern scientific understanding and the enduring wisdom upheld by elders who have preserved traditions despite centuries of suppression. For example, sweat lodge ceremonies, integral to many Native American cultures, have been practiced for centuries as a means of spiritual purification and healing. However, these sacred practices faced significant repression; it wasn't until the passage of the American Indian Religious Freedom Act in 1978 that Native Americans could legally perform their ceremonies without government interference.

For those of us who now have the privilege to sit in these sacred ways, it is important to embody gratitude—not just in thought, but in action. These traditions were carried forward at great cost, through times when practicing them could mean death, torture, or other corporal punishment. Rather than approaching them as something to be "adopted" or "made our own," we can honor their survival by acknowledging those who protected them and by engaging with deep reverence, humility, and respect.

As we walk in integrity—honoring the ancestors of the plant medicines, ceremonies, and traditions that predate the modern world and its major religions—we cultivate a right relationship with our predecessors. In doing so, we do not separate ourselves from them, but rather affirm that we are part of an unbroken lineage of seekers, healers, and stewards of sacred knowledge.

An Esselen elder, Chief Littlebear, once taught me a song that echoes this truth:

> *We are the old people.*
> *We are the new people.*
> *We are the same people.*
> *Stronger than before.*

We are not separate from those who came before us. Their wisdom lives in our breath, our prayers, our rituals. And as we reclaim and reconnect to these ways—not through ownership or dominion, but through deep respect and reciprocity—we strengthen the bridge between past and present, ensuring that these traditions live on with the dignity and honor they deserve.

Reclaiming our sovereignty—whether from trauma, unhealthy attachments, or societal conditioning—requires courageously confronting our deepest wounds, many of which originate in childhood. This formative period is when we learn how the world works, what is socially acceptable, and where we fit into it. If we are raised in environments that suppress pain rather than address it, we grow up normalizing emotional disconnection. By bravely facing our wounds, we not only free ourselves but also lighten the burden of trauma for future generations. When we pair this healing with values that honor the Earth and all life upon it, we empower those who come after us to create a more harmonious future—one rooted in connection, respect, and wholeness.

I commend your courage in undertaking the healing of your inner child. Move at your own pace and seek professional support when needed. While the journey may be challenging, remembering why you are doing this—and who you are doing it for—can make even the most difficult moments more bearable.

Your humble servant of love,

Dr. Gemma Andaya

P.S. As you begin this journey, I invite you to see healing as an act of love—one that brings the past, present, and future into harmony. The path ahead may not always be easy, but as water teaches us, true transformation happens through flow, not force. Healing is not about erasing the past but integrating it into the wholeness of who you are.

The next section offers a sacred perspective on trauma and healing, blending Indigenous wisdom with modern psychology. May it support you as you reclaim the deepest parts of yourself.

A Sacred Perspective on Trauma and Healing

I believe we all come into this world innocent, a blank slate, full of potential and untouched by the weight of life's challenges. As we grow, our experiences shape us, molding our understanding of ourselves and the world around us. Some of these experiences are pleasant and nurturing, creating memories of joy, connection, and love. Others, however, may be jarring, shocking, or traumatic, leaving marks on our sense of safety and identity.

In many Indigenous cultures, water is not just life-giving but also a spiritual force capable of holding and cleansing the energy of our experiences. The concept of *"susto"* in Indigenous Mexican and Central American traditions reflects this understanding—where parts of our soul can become "lost" or trapped in time following a traumatic experience. Healing these spiritual injuries often involves rituals of reconnection, calling the fragmented pieces of ourselves back into wholeness.

There is an old parable, found in Indian and Buddhist traditions, about a woman who carried two large water jars to the river each morning. One jar was whole, but the other had a long, jagged crack down its side. By the time she returned home each day, the cracked jar had lost half its water, leaving a trail of drops along the path.

One day, the cracked jar spoke to the woman and said, "I am so sorry for my flaw. Each day, I fail you."]

Modern psychology mirrors this perspective. Trauma can fragment our sense of self, leaving us disconnected from who we are. As adults, we may find ourselves reacting to challenges in ways that feel disproportionate or out of alignment with our values. These reactions often come from younger parts of ourselves—parts still stuck in the timeline of our past, struggling to protect us from perceived dangers.

Healing is an invitation to gently offer these parts of ourselves the care, compassion, and guidance they lacked at the time of the trauma. It is an act of profound self-love and responsibility, one that allows us to bring those fragmented pieces into the present, to integrate them into our wholeness.

The rituals and reflections in this book honor this sacred process. Just as water cleanses and renews, these practices invite you to flow through your healing journey with grace and courage. Healing is not about erasing the past but about integrating it, creating harmony between your past, present, and future selves. By reconnecting with your inner child, you are weaving together the fragmented threads of your being, stepping fully into your most authentic self.

A Prayer for You

May this journey be one of healing, remembrance, and deep
   integration.
May the path ahead be illuminated, revealing the wisdom that
   has always lived within you.
May you be safely held as you reclaim the pieces of yourself
   that were once lost,
and may each step forward bring you closer to your wholeness.

May you be surrounded by love—by extended hands of support,
   by warm embraces,
by voices that remind you to be kind to yourself and others.
May laughter, joy, and celebration meet you often,
   like sunlight dancing on the surface of water.

May the memories that rise to greet you be held with
   tenderness,
and may you trust that even the painful ones carry gifts.
   For water holds memory, and so do you.
In the depths of your being, the stories of your lineage live on.
May you feel the presence of those who came before you,
walking with you, whispering wisdom through the winds,
guiding you home to yourself.

May your connection to the Earth deepen,
honoring the lands from which your ancestors came,
and the lands that now cradle your becoming.

And when the waters within you stir,
reminding you of all that has been,
may you meet yourself with grace, with compassion, with love.

You are safe. You are supported.
You are seen. You are remembered.
And as you walk this sacred path,
may you always know that you are never alone.

Amen. Aho. O Mateo. Om.

As You Change:
On Growth and Discovery

My dearest child,

As I observe the relentless march of time, I find myself captivated by the profound transformation I see in you with each passing day.

The journey of life is a perpetual voyage of change and growth; no one is exempt from this universal law, and you, my dear, are no exception. Each day, each fleeting moment, I bear witness to a new aspect of your character gently surfacing, like a gemstone being slowly polished to perfection. In my quest to understand you, I find myself trying to decipher the intricacies of your soul as you navigate your way through the intricate labyrinth of life. And in the midst of your continuous evolution, a question often crosses my mind: What will remain constant? What elements of your personality and soul will stand unyielding and steadfast against the relentless winds of change?

The experience of seeing you evolve, of witnessing your gradual growth into the person you're destined to become, fills my heart with an indescribable joy. It is a pure delight to see you wholeheartedly accept and explore the essence of who you are, to see you flourish and blossom into a unique individual, unlike any other. It's akin to watching a flower bloom in slow motion, each petal unfurling in its own time to reveal more and more of its inherent beauty.

I eagerly anticipate the opportunity to continue this journey with you, to watch you embody more and more of your true essence. To witness your transformation is truly one of the greatest privileges and joys of life. The journey is long, and the path is not always clear, but together, we will navigate the highs and lows of this incredible adventure.

Yours truly,

Journal Prompts

Growth is a continuous journey, filled with moments of transformation and self-discovery. As you reflect on this letter, consider the ways you have changed and grown over time. These prompts will guide you in exploring how your inner child perceives and supports your evolution.

Reflect on a time when you felt yourself changing or growing. How did it feel? What did your inner child think of this transformation?

Imagine your inner child witnessing your current growth. What words of encouragement or support might they offer you?

Write a letter to your inner child, describing the person you are becoming. Share the aspects of your childhood self you still carry with you today.

Reflecting on your growth and transformation is an act of honoring your inner child's resilience and courage. By exploring these moments of change, you're not only nurturing your past self but also creating space for future growth. Take pride in your journey so far and trust that you are evolving into the person you are meant to be.

Introduction to Water Blessing Rituals

Throughout history, Indigenous communities around the world have revered water as sacred, recognizing it as the source of life and a symbol of renewal, adaptability, and healing. Our ancestors lived in deep harmony with the Earth's rhythms, honoring the sacred cycles that sustain us. Today, many Indigenous peoples continue to act as guardians of water, standing courageously against environmental threats to protect this life-giving element for future generations.

Movements like "Mni Wiconi" (Water Is Life), led by the Standing Rock Sioux Tribe, have brought global attention to the importance of protecting water from contamination. Their efforts have been joined by over 300 Indigenous nations and allies worldwide, a testament to the collective strength and wisdom of those who honor water's sacredness. Similarly, Anishinaabe water protectors like Autumn Peltier and the Mother Earth Water Walkers have carried forward this message, emphasizing the need for awareness and action.

Beyond North America, Indigenous groups in Bolivia, the Amazon, and other regions continue to defend water as a sacred trust for all of humanity.

These acts of protection and reverence align deeply with the work of healing the inner child. Just as water flows through the Earth, nurturing all it touches, our inner child flows through the timelines of our life, carrying both the wounds of the past and the potential for renewal. By reconnecting with water and honoring it in our daily lives, we can mirror its qualities—becoming teachable, adaptable, and open to healing.

Water blessing rituals invite us to pause, reflect, and reconnect with the sacredness of this element. They are small, intentional practices that align our personal healing with the global movement to honor and protect water. By engaging in these rituals, we not only nurture our inner child but also contribute to the collective consciousness of reverence and gratitude for the waters of the world.

As you embark on this journey, you will find rituals recommended throughout the book, placed after the letters and before the prompts. These rituals are invitations to honor water's sacredness and integrate its wisdom into your daily life. Try incorporating them into your routines and notice how your relationship with water deepens and transforms. May these practices remind you that where water flows, life grows. May they guide you to flow more freely in your relationships, emotions, and dreams, offering healing and renewal to the sacred child within.

Thank You for Choosing Me: You Are an Inspiration

My dearest child,

You are not merely a part of my life, but the light that illuminates it, an invaluable gift that has redefined my existence.

Each time you smile, it radiates a warmth that outshines the sun's rays on a tranquil Sunday morning, filling my world with pure delight. The magic of your smile has the power to invigorate my spirit and brighten the dullest day.

Your tears, like a river breaking through its banks, have the strength to open the floodgates of my heart, stirring within me a surge of compassion and concern, the depths of which I haven't known before.

Your voice is not just sound, but music to my ears. It echoes in my soul like the ethereal touch of a mountaintop reaching up to caress the morning mist. It is a sound that resonates with pure innocence and infinite potential.

And your laughter, oh, your laughter! It has the ability to melt away the weight of my worries and the pain of my past, much like the snow melting from the mountaintops when the first breath of spring arrives. Your laugh is a melody that brings hope and joy, a testament to the purest form of happiness.

What greater joy, what higher honor, could there be than to serve as your guardian on this Earth? To hold your hand as you navigate life's journey, to share in your moments of joy and sorrow, is a blessing I am profoundly grateful for.

Your existence, your love, has inspired me to strive to be better every day. To be kinder in spirit, more patient in adversity, and more tender in my words and actions. Thank you, my precious child, for choosing me, for giving me the privilege to be a part of your life.

Yours truly,

_____

Water Blessing Ritual
Thanking Water Before Drinking

Before you take your next sip of water, pause and reflect on its journey. Envision the streams, rivers, and rain that brought it to you. Place your hands around your glass and speak to the water:

"Thank you for flowing into my being and nourishing my life. May your vitality bring me strength, clarity, and balance."

Drink consciously, feeling gratitude for every drop.

Journal Prompts

The love and inspiration your inner child bring are reminders of their immeasurable worth. Their joy, resilience, and light illuminate your path as you continue to grow. The following prompts will help you reflect on how this connection inspires your life today.

Reflect on the moments when your inner child has inspired, taught, or led you. What are they like in those positions? What is the message they convey to you that helps guide you?

Imagine your inner child thanking you for something. What might they say and how does it feel to hear their gratitude?

Write a love letter to your inner child, thanking them for their presence and the light they bring into your life.

Your inner child's light has inspired you in ways you might only now be recognizing. By expressing gratitude and reflecting on their role in your life, you're deepening this sacred connection. Remember that their joy, creativity, and bravery will always be a source of strength and inspiration for you.

Love Will Remain:
On Resilience and Perseverance

My dearest child,

The journey of life often mirrors the vast ocean, with its serene moments of calm waters interrupted by the crashing waves against the shore. It won't always be an easy path; it won't always be gentle or kind. There will be days when the sun seems to hide behind the clouds, days when the world feels like a stormy sea, relentless and unforgiving.

Just as the ocean shapes the coastline, life has a way of handing us some hardships. These adversities come not to break us, but to mold us, to teach us invaluable lessons, and to strengthen us, turning us into resilient beings capable of withstanding the harshest storms.

In this world, there are very few things I can guarantee. I cannot promise you a journey devoid of pain, a life free of difficulties. I cannot assure you that every day will be filled with sunshine and joy. But there is one thing I can guarantee with unwavering certainty—my love for you will always remain, unchanging and perpetual.

In those dark days, when you feel lost and alone, allow the force of love that is abundantly available to envelop you. Let it be your beacon in the night, leading you back to the path. Allow it to nourish you, to replenish your spirit, to protect you from the biting winds of despair, and to strengthen you, providing you the courage to face another day. Let it be the quiet lullaby that calms your distress, the warm hug that reassures you.

And on those rainy days, when the cold seeps into your bones, let the force of my love bring you warmth. Allow it to be your shield, protecting you from the chill, wrapping you in a cocoon of comfort and security. My love for you will forever remain your comfort, your strength, your shield, your warmth. Always.

Yours truly,

_____

Water Blessing Ritual: Praying or Singing Over Baths/Showers

As you prepare for a bath or shower, treat the water as sacred. Speak, hum, or sing to it, offering gratitude for its ability to cleanse and renew. You might say:

"Sacred water, I honor your power to wash away what is not in alignment with my purpose and mission in this lifetime. May you leave me refreshed, aligned, and renewed in body, mind, and spirit."

As the water flows over you, imagine it carrying away tension, negativity, and old patterns.

Journal Prompts

In times of hardship, your inner child may carry both pain and the seeds of resilience. As you reflect on this letter, consider how you can provide the love and strength your inner child needs to navigate life's challenges. The prompts below will guide you in exploring these themes further.

Recall a challenging time in your life and reflect on how your inner child might have experienced it. What support or love would they have needed during that moment?

Imagine your inner child facing a storm in their life. What words of reassurance can you offer them to remind them of their strength?

Write about a moment when you demonstrated resilience.
As an elder telling a story to the youth to encourage them,
share about this memory with your inner child.

Acknowledging the challenges your inner child has faced is an act of profound love and courage. By reflecting on their resilience, you are helping to heal old wounds and reinforce their strength. Carry this awareness with you and know that your inner child's spirit is always strong enough to weather life's storms.

Who Are YOU?
On Embracing Individuality

My dearest child,

In the world outside, there's a cacophony of voices dictating who you should be, what you should do, and how you should live. I beseech you, pay no attention to it. You are an individual, unique and irreplaceable, not meant to get lost in the crowd or blend into the background. Remember, it takes an immense amount of courage to remain authentically yourself amidst the pressure to conform.

By staying true to yourself, by remaining steadfast in your individuality, you do more than just exist. You inspire, you lead, you encourage those around you to also allow themselves to shine their light on this world. We all have something to share, a unique contribution to make, a singular voice in the grand symphony of life. As your guide and supporter, I aspire to create an environment for you where you can discover these answers. I want you to break free from

generic, cookie-cutter social constraints, to shatter the molds that limit your potential, and to pioneer new territories of thought, action, and existence.

There may be instances in life when you will find yourself breaking through conventional norms and molds, pushing boundaries and stepping outside your comfort zone. In these moments, you might feel like there's a steep price to pay for your actions, possibly experiencing resistance or backlash from those around you. However, as you forge ahead, creating a new path that was previously untraveled, you'll start to see the profound impact of your courage. Over time, your actions will inspire and pave the way for many others to follow in your footsteps, challenging the status quo and making a difference in their own unique way. When you look back, you will realize that, despite the challenges, every step was worth it.

You, my dear, are different. This is your strength, your superpower. Cherish it. For in this difference lies your capacity to effect change, to leave a mark, to make this world a better place. So, ask yourself, what is your message? What is your melody?

Yours truly,

_____

Water Blessing Ritual: Thanking the Rains

When the rains come, take a moment to pause, step outside, or sit near a window. Close your eyes and feel the presence of the rain as it nourishes the Earth. Speak softly or silently:

"Thank you, sacred rain, for replenishing the Earth and bringing life to all that you touch. May your flow bring balance, harmony, and renewal to the land, all sentient beings, and my heart."

Journal Prompts

Your individuality is a gift, a unique light in the world. Your inner child has always carried the seed of who you truly are. These prompts invite you to celebrate that authenticity and to explore ways to honor your inner child's courage to be themselves.

List three unique qualities your inner child possesses. How do those qualities show up in your life now?

Imagine your inner child stepping boldly into the world, fully embracing their individuality. What would they do or say?

Write a dialogue with your inner child about a time when you felt pressured to conform. How can you work together to celebrate your authentic self?

Celebrating your individuality honors the unique magic of your inner child. By exploring their authentic self, you are empowering them to shine without fear. Trust in your ability to embrace and express your true self, knowing that your inner child is always cheering you on.

The World Is Your Oyster: On Dreams and Aspirations

My dearest child,

You are a gem, a treasure more precious than any earthly material. Just by being in this world, you bring joy, and your presence is a gift that cannot be measured. You do not need to be anything other than yourself, for your essence is enough and it's beautiful.

As time gently passes, as the days turn into months and years, we are discovering more about who YOU are. We are gradually peeling back the layers, revealing not just the person you're becoming, but the unique soul you are. We are learning about what invigorates you, what makes your heart sing, and what talents lie within you, waiting to be fully realized and embraced.

As you journey through this process of self-discovery, as

you unravel the gifts that are inherently yours and stumble upon the things that set your soul on fire, don't let the opinions of others dictate what you should make of YOUR life. This is your journey, your path to tread, and your story to write.

Whether your heart leads you toward the arts, where you can express the depths of your emotions and thoughts, or education, where you can quench your thirst for knowledge and perhaps ignite that thirst in others, or the healing arts where you can help the sick in mind, body, and spirit, or business, where you can innovate and create, remember to always follow your heart. From that space of authenticity and passion, magic becomes the norm, and love becomes the vibrant paint that colors the canvas of your life.

And as you walk this path, know this: I am and will always be in your corner. I am your unwavering cheerleader, your vigilant guardian, and your constant prayer. I trust in your choices, I believe in your potential, and I have faith in your journey. Whichever path you choose, I have no doubt that your heart will remain kind, your spirit will remain full of devotion, and your actions will be steeped in the desire to serve others and make a difference.

You are loved, you are cherished, and you are capable of greatness. Remember this always.

Yours truly,

_____

Water Blessing Ritual: Offerings to the Waters

When you find yourself near a natural body of water, offer a small gift in gratitude. Choose something meaningful, such as a crystal, flowers, loose-leaf tobacco, cedar, or incense. Hold the offering in your hands and set an intention:

"I offer this gift to you in reverence and gratitude. Thank you for your life-giving flow. May your wisdom and renewal touch all beings."

Gently place your offering into the water, watching it merge with the currents.

Journal Prompts

Dreams are the language of your inner child, a reflection of their bound-less creativity and potential. As you engage with the following prompts, reflect on how you can reconnect with their dreams and bring some of that magic into your present life.

Think back to a childhood dream or aspiration. What was it and how does it make you feel now? How can you bring some of that dream into your life today?

Reflect on a goal you've achieved as an adult. How would your inner child celebrate this success with you?

What are your inner child's wildest dreams? What would they ask you to do to make those dreams come true?

Dreaming big and reconnecting with your inner child's aspirations is a beautiful way to honor their creativity and spirit. By exploring these dreams, you are opening the door to endless possibilities. Keep believing in your ability to bring their magic into your present and future life.

Protect Your Heart: On Joy and Celebration

My dearest child,

My prayer for you is to find and sustain a sense of joy and celebration in your life. Every moment, from waking to sleeping, may your heart be full of gratitude for it all. May your heart remain:

> Light as a feather, floating effortlessly through the challenges and joys that come your way. Like a bird soaring high in the sky, free from the burdens that could weigh you down.

> Flexible like a bending twig, able to adapt and grow stronger with each bend and twist in your journey. Just as a tree withstands the fiercest winds, may you bend but never break under the pressures of life.

Purify your worries and hurts regularly, as steadfastly as a river cleansing its course, washing away impurities to reveal the clear, sparkling water beneath. Let your spirit be renewed continually, finding clarity and peace in the flow of life.

If and when you are wronged, give forgiveness right away, without hesitation or reservation. Forgiveness is the balm that soothes the hurt, healing wounds and restoring peace to your soul. It is the gentle rain that softens the hardest soil, allowing new life to take root and flourish.

But also protect yourself and your loved ones, standing guard over the precious gems that are your relationships and dreams. Secure the fences around what you've built, ensuring that what you hold dear remains safe and cherished. Be vigilant in your care, yet open your heart to the possibilities of trust and connection.

Let love be your shield and empathy your armor, so that negativity finds no home within you. Through trials and tribulations, as well as excitements and celebrations, I pray your heart remains light and joyful. May your spirit soar high above adversity, finding strength in each challenge and joy in each victory.

Yours truly,

_____

Water Blessing Ritual: Daily Reflection on Water Flow

Water moves through your life in countless ways, from washing your hands to the rivers that run across the Earth. Take a moment to reflect on its role in your day. As you observe the flow of water, say:

"Where water flows, life goes. May I embody your adaptability, moving through life's currents with grace and ease. Thank you for reminding me of my own strength and ability to nourish others."

Journal Prompts

Joy is a sacred gift, and your inner child holds the key to finding it. This letter is a reminder to protect your heart while remaining open to the beauty of life. The prompts that follow will help you explore ways to invite more joy and celebration into your daily experiences.

Imagine your inner child creating a "joy list." What activities, people, or experiences would they include?

Imagine your inner child creating a list of people, places, or experiences that trigger them to feel unsafe. How can you minimize or eliminate exposure to these triggers?

Write a letter to your inner child about the importance of protecting their heart while remaining open to joy. Give them permission and empower them to practice autonomy, consent, and boundaries.

Your reflections on joy and celebration help to safeguard the light within your inner child. By inviting these feelings into your life, you are ensuring that your heart remains open and vibrant. Continue to cherish the moments that bring you joy and protect the sacred essence of your inner child.

One Foot in Front of the Other: On Surrendering to the Process

My dearest child,

Achieving a goal is a journey, a series of steps taken one after another, rather than a singular focus on the ultimate objective. It's a process, a sequence of events that unfolds over time, and it's in this process that you find growth and transformation. Remember to surrender to the journey, accept it in all its forms, and even try to find joy in it. Be kind to yourself and gentle, for it is in the journey that you'll find not just the goal, but also yourself.

We are not striving for something as elusive and illusory as perfection. Perfection, in its traditional sense,

doesn't truly exist. Instead, our aim, our purpose, is to create a beautiful tapestry—a woven masterpiece of all your likes, desires, talents, and dreams. This tapestry, radiant and unique, will bring warmth and comfort not just to you, but also to those around you. It will serve as a testament to the beauty of your journey and the warmth of the Creator.

Picture your life as a magnificent garden. Each step you take is like planting a seed. Some seeds will sprout immediately, while others may take time to bloom. Nurture each one with patience and love, knowing that the process of growth is as important as the final blossom. Even the tiniest buds contribute to the splendor of the entire garden.

As you weave your tapestry, remember that every thread has its purpose. The vibrant colors of your joys, the deep hues of your sorrows, the subtle shades of your daily moments—all contribute to the masterpiece that is your life. Each thread is essential, and together they create a work of art that is uniquely yours.

Instead of being overwhelmed by the grand vision of your destination, focus on taking one step at a time. Just as a hiker ascends a mountain by carefully placing one foot in front of the other, so too should you approach your path. Each step, no matter how small, brings you closer to your goal. Celebrate these steps as they come, for each one is a victory in its own right.

Yours truly,

_____

Water Blessing Ritual: Water As a Vessel for Prayer

When you feel the need to pray deeply, place a glass of water near you—on your altar, bedside, or any sacred space—as you speak your prayers. Water, which holds memory, will carry your intentions. When you are ready, offer the water to a plant, returning your prayer to the Earth and surrendering it to the Creator. In this act of release, listen for the quiet wisdom of what your next step should be.

Journal Prompts

Every journey is made up of small steps, and your inner child understands the value of patience and persistence. As you reflect on this letter, use the prompts to explore how you can support your inner child in focusing on progress rather than perfection.

When anxiety about the future builds, what affirmations can you speak to your inner child and yourself to gently refocus on the present moment? Consider creating a personal mantra—something simple yet grounding, like "One step at a time, I am moving forward" or "I trust the timing of my journey."

What practical steps can you take today to support a calm-
er, more patient approach to achieving your goals?

Each small step you take is a victory worth celebrating. By reflecting on your progress, you are encouraging your inner child to trust the journey and find joy in the process. Carry this awareness forward, knowing that every step brings you closer to your goals and strengthens your connection with your inner child.

An Invitation to Deepen Communication

Dear reader,

This next section invites you to explore the tender emotions your inner child may still carry—the fears and hurts that deserve a voice and compassionate attention, as well as the dreams and joys. Approaching these feelings can be a deeply healing experience, but it can also feel overwhelming at times. Please remember you are in control of this process. Go at your own pace, take breaks when needed, and approach each step with patience and kindness for yourself.

Create a Supportive Environment Before You Begin
Light a candle, hold a comforting object, or spend a few moments breathing deeply to ground yourself. If strong emotions arise, remind yourself that these feelings are a natural part of the healing journey and do not need to overwhelm you. Your adult self is here now—strong, kind, and capable of offering the reassurance and care your inner child may have lacked.

Self-Soothing Practices and Tips for Grounding
As you navigate this journey, it's essential to care for your emotional and physical well-being. Here are a variety of practices to help you stay grounded and support your healing process.

GROUNDING TECHNIQUES

5-4-3-2-1 grounding exercise: Use your senses to connect with the present moment.

- Name 5 things you can see.

- Name 4 things you can feel.

- Name 3 things you can hear.

- Name 2 things you can smell.

- Name 1 thing you can taste.

Connecting to nature: If possible, step outside. Touch the ground with bare feet, hold a rock or leaf, or simply take a moment to observe the sky.

CREATIVE EXPRESSION

Art journaling: Use colors, shapes, and imagery to express what words cannot. Even simple doodles can provide relief.

Music for healing: Listen to calming music or sounds of nature. Singing or humming can also help regulate your nervous system.

BODY AWARENESS

Movement and release: Shake or stretch your body to release stagnant energy that may surface during these dialogues. Movement helps your nervous system reset and allows emotions to flow more freely.

Progressive muscle relaxation: Focus on tensing and then relaxing each muscle group in your body, starting at your toes and moving upward.

Self-soothing touch: Place your hand over your heart or hug yourself gently. This physical act can signal safety and comfort to your nervous system.

Visualization: Imagine a safe and peaceful place where your inner child can feel free and secure. Describe this place in detail or sketch it.

Gratitude reflection: Write down three things you're grateful for after each journaling session to balance emotional release with positive reflection.

Mantras and affirmations: Repeat calming phrases to yourself, such as:

- "My body is responding to the past, but I am safe now."

- "I am strong enough to feel these emotions and let them pass."

- "I am not alone. I am loved and supported."

Rituals for Closure

Closing the session: At the end of each journaling session, say or write a closing affirmation, such as, "I honor my courage and release what no longer serves me."

Cleansing with water: Wash your hands or face with intention, imagining the water cleansing away any residual tension or emotional heaviness.

Why These Practices Work

- Grounding anchors you to the present, reducing feelings of being overwhelmed or stuck in past memories.

- Movement and touch release stress and help your body find relaxation and safety.

- Creative expression allows emotions to flow in a nonverbal and cathartic way.

- Closure rituals signal to your mind and body that the process is complete for now, promoting peace and calm.

When to Seek Professional Support

Some experiences and emotions may feel too heavy or confusing to process alone. Here are a few signs that you might benefit from the support of a trauma-informed therapist or counselor:

- Experiencing flashbacks or feeling like you're reliving past events.

- Having intrusive thoughts or recurring memories that disrupt daily life.

- Feeling stuck in mental loops, replaying the same thoughts or events without resolution.

- Experiencing uncontrollable emotions—such as intense sadness, anger, or fear—when thinking about certain experiences.

- Struggling with lashing out at loved ones or difficulty maintaining relationships due to unresolved pain.

If you notice any of these signs, consider reaching out to a professional who can guide you through this journey in a safe and structured way.

There is strength in seeking support, and you do not have to face this alone.

Above all, be gentle with yourself. This is a process of uncovering, releasing, and ultimately healing. You are already brave for taking this step, and you are not alone.

Yours truly,

Dr. Gemma Andaya

The Inner Child Speaks:
Guided Prompts

Reconnecting with Your Inner Child

When you think of your child, what age do you see them? What are they wearing and doing? What is their body language like? Where are they?

As you focus on your child, you start to sense their emotions and their thoughts. What have they been longing to ask or understand?

What response do you have for your child? Please note this is an opportunity to reparent them and give them elder wisdom they need to hear. Speak to them as a child who just needs some unconditional love and encouragement, not critically or instructionally.

How can you remind your inner child that they are never alone and will always have your love and protection? Write them a love letter.

What promises can you make to your inner child to nurture, honor, and listen to them moving forward?

How can you remind your inner child that they are never alone and will always have your love and protection?

Create a safe space for your inner child in your imagination. Describe what it looks like, feels like, and what you both do together in this space.

Giving Your Inner Child a Voice

Imagine your inner child sitting with you. What are they most afraid to share? Write their feelings down without judgment or pressure.

Reflect on a time when your inner child felt misunderstood or unseen. What would you say to them now to reassure them they are valued and loved?

Ask your inner child, "What made you feel scared or hurt as a child?" Listen to their response and offer them compassion through your words. How can you, as the adult, help them release or transform this burden?

Write a letter from your inner child to someone who caused them pain, expressing their feelings openly and honestly. (This letter is for your healing; you do not need to share it with anyone.)

Reflect on how you've been a protector for your inner child. Are there ways you can show up more consistently for them?

Letting Your Inner Child Guide You

Ask your inner child, "What would make life more fun and magical for us right now?" Write down their response as if they're speaking directly to you.

What dreams or creative ideas did you have as a child that you've set aside? Explore how those ideas could be reimagined in your adult life.

If your inner child could plan the perfect day for you, what would it look like? Write about the activities, feelings, and experiences they'd choose.

Imagine your inner child writing a letter to your future self. What wisdom or advice do they offer about living with joy and authenticity?

Reflect on one area of your life where you feel stuck. What perspective or solution does your inner child offer to help you move forward?

Final Closure Ritual:
Flowing into Wholeness

As we close this sacred process, let us turn to water—the element of the South—to guide us in honoring the work we have done and inviting its wisdom to flow into our lives. This ritual is an opportunity to deepen your connection with the South and your inner child, while embracing the qualities of water: adaptability, renewal, and emotional clarity.

The Ritual

1. **Find a Natural Body of Water:** Seek out a natural body of water that feels meaningful to you—a lake, creek, river, waterfall, or ocean. If you cannot physically access water, create a sacred space at home with a bowl of clean water to represent this element.

2. **Connect with the Water:** Approach the water with intention, acknowledging its presence as a living, sacred force. Speak to the water directly, expressing your gratitude and respect. You might say: *"Thank you for your life-giving flow, your adaptability, and your ability to cleanse and renew. I honor your presence and ask for your wisdom as I continue my journey of healing."*

3. **Make an Offering:** Prepare an offering that feels sacred to you. This could be loose-leaf tobacco, cedar, copal, flowers, or something personal like jewelry or a crystal. Honor your own traditions,

religions, or lineage by choosing an offering that reflects your heart. With care, release the offering into the water while saying: *"I give this offering as a symbol of my gratitude and as a request for your guidance. May your qualities flow through my life, helping me grow and heal."*

4. **Pray for Water Qualities to Infuse Your Being:** Take a moment to pray or reflect, inviting the qualities of water to infuse your life. Speak aloud or silently:

   · "May I embody water's adaptability, flowing through challenges with ease."

   · "May water's clarity cleanse my subconscious and bring me emotional balance."

   · "May water's wisdom guide my relationships, my *dreams, and my tools for navigating this life."*

5. **Close with a Sacred Bathing or Anointing:** If it is safe and possible, immerse yourself in the water to complete the ritual, symbolizing renewal and integration. Allow the water to cleanse and bless your body, mind, and soul. If immersion isn't possible, gather water in your hands and gently anoint yourself on your:

   · **Crown** (for clarity of thought and connection to spirit)

   · **Third eye** (for intuitive wisdom)

   · **Throat** (for truth and authentic expression)

   · **Heart** (for emotional balance and compassion) As you anoint, reflect on the journey you've undertaken and the growth you've experienced.

Final Words

When the ritual feels complete, take a moment to thank the water for its presence and support. Leave the space as you found it, honoring its sacredness. As you walk away, carry the qualities of water with you, trusting in your ability to flow through life with grace and adaptability.

Epilogue: Flowing Forward

Water teaches us that healing is not linear but cyclical, always moving and adapting. Some days, your flow may feel like a rushing river; other days, like a still pond. Trust in the process and honor the rhythm of your unique journey. This work you've done—reconnecting with your inner child, exploring their fears, joys, and wisdom—is an incredible act of love. But the relationship you've cultivated with your inner child does not end here. It is something to be nurtured and tended to regularly, just as we nurture the most important relationships in our lives.

To support you as you integrate the lessons and insights from this book, here are a few practices to carry forward.

1. Honor the "'Why" and the "What"

It is valuable to understand why you are the way you are. Your past, your experiences, and your inner child's journey have shaped you. Honor this understanding with compassion—it is a vital part of your story. But healing also requires you to take action in the present. Reflect on the *"what:"*

- What will you do now to create change?

- What steps will you take to honor your inner child and bring their needs into your adult life?

Growth is a balance of acknowledgment and action, reflection and movement.

2. Stay Connected to Your Inner Child

The relationship with your inner child is ongoing and dynamic. They will continue to need your love, support, and presence as you move through life. Reflect on the signs that your inner child might need your attention:

- Are you feeling unusually reactive, emotional, or defensive?

- Are you experiencing physical tension or discomfort that feels familiar but unexplainable?

- Is your environment presenting cues or triggers that remind you of old wounds?

These moments are invitations to check in with your inner child, to listen, and to offer them comfort and guidance. Staying attuned to these cues ensures that the connection remains strong and supportive.

3. Revisit and Reflect

Healing is a layered process, and there will always be more to discover. Return to these prompts, letters, and reflections at a later time to see if anything new wants to be expressed. With time, the insights you gain may deepen and new perspectives may emerge.

- Set aside moments of reflection periodically to ask: What does my inner child need now? How have we grown since we last connected?

This ongoing dialogue ensures that the relationship continues to evolve as you do.

4. Share Your Journey with Discernment

Healing journeys are deeply personal, but they can also inspire and empower others. When it feels right, share your experiences with trusted individuals. Whether it's with a friend, a counselor, or a community, talking about your inner child work can:

- Help you feel less alone in your journey.

- Provide new insights from the perspectives of others.

- Inspire someone else to embark on their own path of healing.

That said, practice discernment. Sharing requires a safe space and individuals who can hold your story with care. Your inner child deserves protection and respect, even as you open yourself to connection with others.

Carrying the spirit of the South

The South teaches us to be like water—adaptive, resilient, and ever-flowing. It invites us to remain teachable, open to growth, and rooted in the essence of the child. Carry this spirit forward as you continue your journey of healing and integration. Just as water carves new paths and brings life to all it touches, your work with your inner child has the power to transform not only your own life but also the lives of those around you.

You are the sacred caretaker of your own soul, and this work is a profound act of self-love and self-responsibility. By tending to your inner child, you are reclaiming your wholeness, one moment at a time.

With gratitude for your courage,

Dr. Gemma Andaya

www.ingramcontent.com/pod-product-compliance
Lightning Source LLC
Chambersburg PA
CBHW041157120626
46547CB00020B/3250